S0-BYV-781

SEEK

By
PAUL FLEISCHMAN

Dramatic Publishing
Woodstock, Illinois • England • Australia • New Zealand

*** NOTICE ***

The amateur and stock acting rights to this work are controlled exclusively by THE DRAMATIC PUBLISHING COMPANY without whose permission in writing no performance of it may be given. Royalty must be paid every time a play is performed whether or not it is presented for profit and whether or not admission is charged. A play is performed any time it is acted before an audience. Current royalty rates, applications and restrictions may be found at our Web site: www.dramaticpublishing.com, or we may be contacted by mail at: DRAMATIC PUBLISHING COMPANY, P.O. Box 129, Woodstock IL 60098.

COPYRIGHT LAW GIVES THE AUTHOR OR THE AUTHOR'S AGENT THE EXCLUSIVE RIGHT TO MAKE COPIES. This law provides authors with a fair return for their creative efforts. Authors earn their living from the royalties they receive from book sales and from the performance of their work. Conscientious observance of copyright law is not only ethical, it encourages authors to continue their creative work. This work is fully protected by copyright. No alterations, deletions or substitutions may be made in the work without the prior written consent of the publisher. No part of this work may be reproduced or transmitted in any form or by any means, electronic or mechanical, including photocopy, recording, videotape, film, or any information storage and retrieval system, without permission in writing from the publisher. It may not be performed either by professionals or amateurs without payment of royalty. All rights, including, but not limited to, the professional, motion picture, radio, television, videotape, foreign language, tabloid, recitation, lecturing, publication and reading, are reserved.

For performance of any songs, music and recordings mentioned in this play which are in copyright, the permission of the copyright owners must be obtained or other songs and recordings in the public domain substituted.

©MMVI by
PAUL FLEISCHMAN
Printed in the United States of America
All Rights Reserved
(SEEK)

ISBN: 1-58342-382-6

IMPORTANT BILLING AND CREDIT REQUIREMENTS

All producers of the Play *must* give credit to the Author of the Play in all programs distributed in connection with performances of the Play and in all instances in which the title of the Play appears for purposes of advertising, publicizing or otherwise exploiting the Play and/or a production. The name of the Author *must* also appear on a separate line, on which no other name appears, immediately following the title, and *must* appear in size of type not less than fifty percent the size of the title type. Biographical information on the Author, if included in the playbook, may be used in all programs. *In all programs this notice must appear:*

Produced by special arrangement with
THE DRAMATIC PUBLISHING COMPANY of Woodstock, Illinois

PRODUCTION NOTES

Seek is a play for voices, performed by speakers playing multiple parts. Since radio figures prominently in the story, the play can be staged as a live radio broadcast, with speakers gathered around microphones on a set suggesting a radio studio. More simply, the speakers could approach podiums or lit areas to speak, with touches from Rob's world sprinkled about the stage: A shortwave radio, world map, an accordion, a Giants cap. The set could also recreate Rob's building, with his grandparents on one side and he and his mother on the other, perhaps at different heights. Having fewer speaking areas than speakers provides movement, as actors approach and retreat. For a less static look, the whole stage could be a speaking area, with the actors using it unpredictably, forming scene groupings that then dissolve, perhaps recreating the circular Whispering Gallery at the opening and closing. Lighting can be used to highlight speakers, moving the audience's focus around the stage.

To help the audience keep track of who's talking, the roles of Rob, Boy Rob, and Rob's mother should be read by actors playing no other roles. The other parts can be handled by a cast as large or small as the director sees fit. Though speakers could memorize their lines, they needn't, especially if the play is presented as a radio broadcast. Audiences have quickly accepted the sight of actors reading off the page, and have seemed not to miss costumes, set changes, and physical action.

The intermission can be omitted and the play performed straight through if desired.

SEEK

A Play in Two Acts
For a minimum of 4m., 4w.
May be expanded to as many as 18m., 17w.

CHARACTERS

Males

Rob, 17
Rob's Grandfather
Male Radio Announcer
Mr. McCarthy
Lenny, 22
Boy Rob, ages 8-12
Audiobook Reader
1st Baseball Announcer
2nd Baseball Announcer
Nick
Male Caller, 40
Ray, 40
Zad
Coach
Male Student
Dean
Male Writer
Andy

Females

Rob's Mother, 45
Rob's Grandmother
Exercise Video Host
Aunt June
Spanish TV Actress
Aunt Jessica
Mrs. Kathos, 60
Teacher
Female Radio Announcer
Female Caller
English Teacher
Female Student
Mrs. Druckenmuller, 60
Female Writer
Penelope
Neva
Old Woman

SEEK was given its premiere September 14, 2001, as a radio broadcast before a live audience at the Santa Rosa Central Library in Santa Rosa, Calif., simultaneously broadcast on station KRCB. The performance was produced by Cathy Signorelli, Robin Pressman and Bruce Robinson. It was directed by Walter M. Mayes, with sound design by Ted Crimy. The cast was:

Rob	Steve Rexrode
Boy Rob	Anthony Mayes
Rob's Mother	Corisa Aaronson
Rob's Grandmother	Joan Coleman
Rob's Grandfather	Basil Coleman
Aunt June, Mrs. Druckenmuller	Susan Rexrode
Aunt Jessica, English Teacher	Victoria Brown
Lenny	Tom Viers
Mr. McCarthy, Mrs. Kathos, Ray, Coach, Dean, Andy	Kernan Coleman
Zad, Nick, Male Writer, Teacher	Bruce Edelstein
Penelope	Abigail Heidbreder
Neva	Taylor Anderson-Stevenson
Radio Voices	Kernan Coleman, Abigail Heidbreder, Walter M. Mayes, Corisa Aaronson, Victoria Brown

ACT ONE

(We hear a recording of swamp sounds: frogs croaking, birds calling, water rippling gently. It has a night feel, soothing and mysterious. We hear a different portion of it each time it recurs. It fades out after ten seconds.)

ROB. Remember, Mom, when we went to London?

ROB'S MOTHER. Sure.

ROB. The day we went to St. Paul's Cathedral?

ROB'S MOTHER. Of course I do, Rob.

ROB'S GRANDMOTHER *(reading)*. "The elevator operator was a skinny redhead with more lipstick than lips. 'Well, Mr. Brindle,' she said. 'You're an early bird this morning.' He stubbed out his cigarette. 'I've got a date with a worm.'"

ROB. Remember climbing all those stairs to get up to the dome?

ROB'S MOTHER. Hundreds of them. *Thousands* of them.

ROB'S GRANDFATHER. Boys your age, Robbie, working in the coal mines. Nine-year-old girls in the textile mills.

ROB. And remember, there was a walkway around the inside of the dome?

ROB'S MOTHER. Sure I remember. The Whispering Gallery.

AUNT JUNE *(reading)*. "Slate-black except for white belly and outer tail feathers. Catches insects on wing, hunting from perch. Voice: a thin, strident *FEE-bee*."

MALE RADIO ANNOUNCER. This is HCJB, the voice of the Andes, broadcasting from Quito, Ecuador—

ROB. Remember how voices moved around the dome, so you could hear what someone was saying way across on the other side?

ROB'S MOTHER. And then that whole class of school kids came up, all talking at once.

SPANISH TV ACTRESS. *Te juro, mi vida. ¡Te amo! ¡Con todo mi corazón, te amo!*

ROB. That's what it's like in my head. Exactly. Voices bouncing everywhere.

MR. McCARTHY *(reading)*. "—will serve as your senior thesis in English. Like the autobiographies we've read this year, yours should probe the themes in your life, analyzing signal events and charting the influences of family, community, and your historical era on your development. All information will be treated as strictly confidential. On the brink of your departure from high school, this is a chance for you to look back and use both your literary and critical thinking skills—"

ROB. Ever since McCarthy gave us the assignment.

MALE RADIO ANNOUNCER. Two on, two out. The Giants really need a hit here.

ROB. Except instead of looking back, it's like I keep...listening back.

(Here, as later, the swamp sounds come up, playing before, during and briefly after the excerpt from LENNY's tape.)

LENNY. It's eleven o'clock at Oldies-93. Another Tuesday night, I'm Lenny Guidry, and it's request time. A little show we call the "The Ghost Raising." Most appropriate at this Halloween time. You know what trick-or-treating's really about? Making the dead one's favorite foods. That's what brings 'em back home. Down in Mexico, at Day of the Dead, they bring the meal right there to the cemetery. For my old ones, I always make gumbo. That's why I was driving all over the whole Bay Area yesterday looking for okra. Put another hundred miles on Anne-Marie, who's already got three hundred thousand on her and arthritis in both axles, but you just can't make gumbo without okra. What do you do if it's not Halloween and you got somebody you want to bring back? You call me up right here and leave a message about what you want to hear. 'Cause music works as good as food. Brings back the old times and the old folks. Makes your wallpaper change right there on the wall to what you had when you were a baby, or maybe to when you and your sweetie first met. So let's turn back the clock and raise a few ghosts. Maestro, the message machine.

ROB'S GRANDFATHER. So the longshoremen decided to go on strike. They stopped loading and unloading ships and they blocked the docks with picket lines. You know about the Fourth of July. But did they teach you in school about the *fifth* of July, Robbie?

ROB *(reading)*. "Autobiography of Robert A. Radkovitz. By Robert A. Radkovitz... Part One... Chapter One... Preface... I grew up in a house built of voices."

ROB'S GRANDFATHER. The fifth of July is famous in San Francisco. It's called "Bloody Thursday," because that's when the big businessmen—

BOY ROB. Are they the bad guys?

ROB'S GRANDFATHER. Right. Very bad. So bad that they paid for scabs to drive trucks right into the line of strikers, right down there at Pier 38.

BOY ROB. I have a scab. On my elbow. Look.

ROB'S GRANDFATHER. Grandpa sees. But this kind of scab is different. It's a man who doesn't belong to a union. Grandpa sees. Remember unions? They're like a team. Grandpa sees, Robbie. Put your arm down now.

ROB *(reading)*. "Neither of my grandparents could be described as sugar-sweet or marooned in easy chairs. My grandfather was and is a history professor at U.C. Berkeley, specializing in labor history. He may be the very first to attempt teaching it to a six-year-old."

ROB'S GRANDMOTHER *(reading)*. "'And Lady Emma, it may interest you to know, has not been taking painting lessons in London, but rather has been visiting a doctor tucked well out of view in Lambeth.' 'Good God! Abortion?' 'Worse,' Marston replied. 'Syphilis.'"

ROB'S GRANDFATHER. Doris—the kid's only in kindergarten!

ROB'S GRANDMOTHER. Yes, dear, I know. But he so loves being read to.

ROB'S GRANDFATHER. He loves it? He's *asleep*!

BOY ROB. No I'm not.

ROB'S GRANDMOTHER. You see.

ROB'S GRANDFATHER. Well, he oughta be. How's he supposed to keep the barristers separate from the solicitors, or understand why the rector's blackmailing the vicar? They don't get to blackmail till sixth grade.

ROB'S GRANDMOTHER. The sense is for me. The *sound* of the language is what he's getting.

ROB *(reading)*. "Books are something I hear, courtesy of my grandmother. She's a vocal quick-change artist: narrator, chimney-sweep, murderer, maid. Mysteries are her dessert. She reads constantly, and did so for a living: proofreader, newspaper copyeditor, then editor at publishing houses. I've seen her read the dictionary for an hour. When I opened it to look up a word, it was my grandmother's voice I always heard in my head."

ROB'S GRANDMOTHER *(reading)*. "Pubis: That part of either innominate bone that, with the corresponding part of the other, forms the front of the pelvis."

ROB *(reading)*. "Even if I didn't want to."

ROB'S MOTHER. Good night, angel.

BOY ROB. No—in French.

ROB'S MOTHER. *Bonne nuit, mon ange.*

ROB *(reading)*. "My mother teaches high-school Spanish and French and also speaks Italian and some German."

BOY ROB. Now say "sweet dreams."

ROB'S MOTHER. *Fais de beaux rêves.*

BOY ROB. How do you *do* that?

ROB *(reading)*. "When we go to the opera, she doesn't need to read the translation. She writes poetry and has kept a journal for more than twenty years. She belongs to a writer's group that meets once a month at our—"

SPANISH TV ACTRESS. *Canalla! Déjame! Este momento!*

ROB *(reading)*. "I used to love the Spanish soap operas she watched to keep up with the language."

BOY ROB. Why's she so mad at him?

ROB'S MOTHER. Well, he married two different women at the same time. This one, and that one in the very tight dress.

BOY ROB. He forgot?

SPANISH TV ACTRESS. *Que los testículos se te asen en el infierno! Y que las cabras orinen sobre tu tumba!*

BOY ROB. What did she just say?

ROB'S MOTHER. That she hoped his testicles will roast in Hell and that goats will pee on his grave.

ROB *(reading)*. "I learned more from them than from health class, psychology class, and the dictionary combined."

MALE RADIO ANNOUNCER. —from Kenosha, Wisconsin, has sent a question she hopes will stump our Opera Quiz panel. "Lohengrin," she writes, "makes his famous entrance in a boat pulled by a swan. But large freshwater birds have played a part in a number of other operas. Listen to the following—"

ROB *(reading)*. "Not having siblings, I was raised among adults and treated as one. It's as if they couldn't wait for me to catch up to them—to history and opera and politics and Lord Peter Whimsey—and so they didn't."

ROB'S GRANDMOTHER. And frankly, dear, I'd much rather he be exposed to the prose style of Agatha Christie than Karl Marx. Marx really had no ear for dialogue.

ROB *(reading)*. "My grandparents' house is a Victorian on Potrero Hill. It was divided vertically into a duplex before they bought it. My mother and I moved into the right side when I was a baby and she needed a place. Since my grandparents helped take care of me when I was little, we put in a connecting door on the second floor for convenience. My mother preferred it closed for privacy, but I liked all the different voices coming from—"

MALE RADIO ANNOUNCER. Coming up on KPFA, "Delano Diary," a radio portrait of the United Farm Workers' historic grape boycott and a look at its long-term—

EXERCISE VIDEO VOICE. Keep it going, keep it going, this is gonna tone your quads *and* your glutes, so you're really killing two flabs with one—

AUDIOBOOK READER. It was half past five before Holmes returned. He was bright, eager, and in excellent spirits.

SPANISH TV ACTRESS. *Maléfico! No me digas mas!*

ROB'S GRANDFATHER *(reading)*. "This patently asinine view of free trade, so beloved by the well-heeled dimwits who bankroll your dismal newspaper—"

ROB *(reading)*. "—the Saturday opera on the radio, my grandfather reading his never-published letters to the editor, the writer's group reading poems and stories, the Giants games I listened to in the evenings—"

1st BASEBALL ANNOUNCER. I mean a *huge* gap between first and second. If Butler could manage to poke one through, and Thompson and Clark could somehow get on—

2nd BASEBALL ANNOUNCER. —that would bring the tying run to the plate.

ROB. "—the announcers openly rooting for the home team, concocting improbable comebacks, willing balls to stay fair or go foul."

1st BASEBALL ANNOUNCER. A lazy fly to center. GOO-tee-air-ez under it—

ROB'S MOTHER. *Goo-TYER-ez!*

ROB *(reading)*. "—and mercilessly mangling the Spanish names."

1st BASEBALL ANNOUNCER. He squeezes it for out number two. That brings JIM-a-nez to the plate.

ROB'S MOTHER. *Hi-MAY-nez!* Can you believe that? I swear I'm going to write a letter to the team.

ROB'S GRANDFATHER. A letter? Good luck, Rose! Here's a stamp. Be my guest!

ROB'S GRANDMOTHER *(reading)*. "It was the best of times, it was the worst of times. It was the age of wisdom, it was the age of foolishness."

AUNT JUNE. "Two white wing-bars, partial eye-ring." Robbie—that's it. A Hutton's vireo!

ROB *(reading)*. "My two wonderful aunts were there a lot, my mother's sisters, neither of them with kids of their own: June, the biologist who took me birdwatching, and Jessica, a teacher who knew boys love big trucks and who drove me on Saturdays to construction sites."

AUNT JESSICA. Look—a grader!

BOY ROB. Wow!

AUNT JESSICA. Man, it's huge! Check out that blade. We are *so lucky*!

ROB'S GRANDMOTHER *(reading)*. "It was the season of light, it was the season of darkness."

ROB *(reading)*. "Next door there were our old Greek neighbors, Mr. and Mrs. Kathos, who treated me like their own grandchild and overpaid me for the simplest chore with square after square of sweet baklava."

MRS. KATHOS. That's enough sweeping, Robbie. You sit now and eat.

ROB'S GRANDFATHER. Let me get this straight. They're paying you with *pastry*? What the hell kind of wage is that?

MR. McCARTHY *(reading)*. "You may wish to interview relatives or other significant figures in your life. Like autobiographers before you, you can draw upon letters, journals, diaries, memorabilia—"

ROB *(reading)*. "Everybody wanted me. I was respected and courted and adored."

ROB'S MOTHER, GRANDPARENTS, AUNTS *(singing)*.
    Happy Birthday to you,
    Happy Birthday to you—

ROB *(reading)*. "I was also dissatisfied. No matter how loudly they sang, I knew there was a voice missing from the chorus. My father's voice."

ROB'S GRANDMOTHER *(reading)*. "It was the spring of hope, it was the winter of despair, we had everything before us, we had nothing before us—"

ROB *(reading)*. "Somehow, that missing voice seemed to outweigh all those that were present. By the time I was seven or eight, I'd made up my mind. I would find him."

ROB'S GRANDMOTHER. Now make a wish.

ROB'S GRANDFATHER. Think about it.

AUNT JESSICA. Take your time.

AUNT JUNE. That was fast. The kid knows what he wants.

ROB'S GRANDPARENTS. And look at him blow!

(We hear the swamp sounds before, during and after LENNY's excerpt.)

LENNY. The Beatles doing "Yesterday" for another satisfied customer here on "The Ghost Raising." Lenny here with you till one a.m. Next up, risking excommunication from the AM airwaves for playing anything longer than three minutes—but also knowing the station manager never listens to the show—by request from a seriously homesick Russian cabdriver, we're gonna hear the entire first movement of the Tchaikovsky Fifth Symphony—

ROB *(reading)*. "I'm a night person. I was formerly a night
boy, and before that a night baby. I was born at night—
three twenty-two a.m. Night's my hometown, the place
I'm comfortable. The sun is so bright it hides. The con-
stellations are always there above us, but can only be
seen after dark. Day-submerged sounds come out with
the stars: crickets in the grass, a piano half a block
away, the car-trailing-tin-cans clatter of a river heard
from a cabin. Moths, the night's butterflies, emerge, pol-
linating the night-blooming flowers. And most important: radio waves travel farther at night."

ROB'S MOTHER. We were so incredibly young, both of
us. I was young, and Lenny was younger. Remember
"The Jumblies," the Edward Lear poem? When you
were little, you could recite the whole—

BOY ROB. "They went to sea in a Sieve, they did,
    In a Sieve they went to sea."

BOY ROB AND ROB.
    "In spite of all their friends could say,
    On a winter's morn, on a stormy day—"

ROB'S MOTHER. I'd hear those first words, and I'd think:
That was us.

ROB. How old were you when you met?

ROB'S MOTHER. I was twenty-five, just finishing my
teaching credential. He was twenty-two. He'd worked at
music stores and radio stations, playing accordion for
dances. Then he decided to see the world outside Louisiana. He had a red Volvo station wagon. He drove all
over the country for six months, pulled into Berkeley,
liked the feel, and stayed. I've told you all this, in
slightly different words.

BOY ROB. Did he go to college with you?

ROB'S MOTHER. No, honey. Your daddy was a musician. Some musicians don't learn at a school. They learn from other musicians. Daddy didn't have notebooks and pencils and books. He had records.

AUNT JESSICA. Like about a ton of 'em in the back of that car. Remember, June? The rear bumper, I swear, was kissing the ground.

AUNT JUNE. Good old Anne-Marie. Something wrong with that engine. I always knew when you guys were coming 'cause you could hear that car six blocks away. Kind of like the train.

AUNT JESSICA. Kind of like the Concorde.

ROB. So how did you meet? The real story, now that I'm not five anymore.

ROB'S MOTHER. He'd hooked up with a fiddler and was playing in a little club on Telegraph that had a dance floor. Some friends and I went. Cajun dancing was just catching on. They played a string of fast songs and then let the dancers catch their breath with a waltz. The waltz was "Little Black Eyes." And I fell in love—with the song and with him. When that happens, you find a way to make contact. In old movies, you see women drop their handkerchiefs.

ROB. And you guys?

ROB'S MOTHER. He borrowed my jumper cables. Two weeks after that, he moved in.

ROB. What was he like?

ROB'S MOTHER. Well... Kind of like the Cajun brochure come to life. Dark-haired and handsome. Moustache. Loved eating. Knew where every milligram of meat was hiding in a crab. He was a night owl—a gene he slipped to you. An unbelievable ear for music. You could pull

out any album in his collection, play just two seconds of
some scratchy field recording of some long-dead-and-
buried Cajun fiddler who sounded like every other Cajun
fiddler, and he'd tell you exactly who was playing and
with whom. He was sociable on the surface but really he
was solitary. He burrowed into his music and was gone.
It was like he was communing with the old guys on his
records, somewhere back on the bayous. A place I could
never go with him.

TEACHER. Richard receives twenty dollars for his birthday and spends five dollars on video games. Laura also
receives twenty dollars for her birthday—

ROB *(reading)*. "Like Richard and Laura in math problems,
like the Valdez family in our Spanish book, my father
was a character, constructed out of words, not flesh."

BOY ROB *(reading)*. "The capital of Louisiana is Baton
Rouge. Its state flower is the magnolia. Its—"

ROB. So what happened?

ROB'S MOTHER. Well, he moved in. And he stayed. I'd
never had a live-in boyfriend before. I felt I was finally
an adult, like my official card had come in the mail. We
were a couple. Rose and Lenny. Lenny and Rose. Invita-
tions came in both of our names. People wrote us in
their address books together. It's so confirming to be
part of a couple. We moved to a tiny house on Pan-
oramic, in the Berkeley hills. A woodstove in the living
room for heat, a bathroom sink you could barely fit both
hands in. He'd play accordion out on this redwood stump
while I cooked or studied. I couldn't see him out there,
but I loved hearing him, hearing his presence. I got my
credential and my first job, part time. Lenny was playing

weekends and had DJ jobs. We were happy. We were in
love. I smiled for two years. And then I got pregnant.

ROB. I was an accident?

ROB'S MOTHER. Not really. Not in my mind. We loved
each other. I didn't see why it should ever end. So it felt
natural to move on to the next stage. Or it did to me.
Lenny saw it a little differently. We had a big fight. Instead of being overjoyed, he slept at a friend's for a week.

MALE RADIO ANNOUNCER. As Act Two of *Madame
Butterfly* opens, three years have passed since Pinkerton's departure.

ROB'S MOTHER. I felt ready for a child. I was twenty-
five. I knew I'd make a good mother. Somewhere I
crossed a line, like crossing the equator—invisible, but
real. The arguments changed from "If we have a baby"
to "When the baby comes." Lenny noticed. And he
knew he wasn't ready. Which he wasn't. He knew himself. I was the one who'd misjudged. I told him I'd go it
alone if I had to. One day I came home from work —I
was in my fifth month—and all his things were gone.

ROB'S GRANDFATHER. I never liked accordions anyway. Or accordion players.

BOY ROB. How come everyone hates accordions?

ROB'S GRANDFATHER. It's called good taste.

ROB. What did you do, after he left?

ROB'S MOTHER. I cried for two days. Then I cleaned
house, repainted, and went out and bought a cradle I
couldn't afford. I'd lost Lenny, but I was about to get
you. I had a great midwife. Eleven hours of labor. When
they finally gave you to me, I looked down at your
eyes—so dark and shiny—and I heard "Little Black
Eyes" in my head. And I started crying.

BOY ROB. "And when the sieve turned round and round
and everyone cried 'You'll all be drowned!'"

AUNT JESSICA. You? You were positively edible, the
cutest baby on the planet. I was so happy to be your
aunt. Suddenly, I was ready for kids. But Nick was still
pretty undecided. I had him take you to baseball games.
Sort of a trial offer.

ROB. Yeah, I remember.

BOY ROB. I have to go to the bathroom.

NICK. What?

BOY ROB. I need to go to the bathroom.

NICK. Now?

BOY ROB. Yeah.

NICK. Are you kidding? The bases are loaded! You
don't—you don't want to miss what happens, do you?

BOY ROB. I need to pee. Really bad.

NICK. Christ, I don't believe it. *We're not missing this.*

BOY ROB. But I need to go.

NICK. Fine! Pee in this.

BOY ROB. But there's still popcorn in it.

ROB. You know what I like? That you didn't make me
hate him. His photo was up on my wall. We talked
about him.

ROB'S MOTHER. Of course we talked. You needed some
answers.

ROB. Did he ever see me?

ROB'S MOTHER. He called June after you were born and
asked your name and birthday. Never visited, never called.
He was still working at an oldies station—I used to listen just to check. Then, maybe six months later, I walked
in the door, and he'd been there. Lying in the cradle was
the sound-effects record. On top of it was the "Ghost

Raising" tape. As soon as I saw, I had a feeling he was gone. Which he was. I called the station and they told me he'd quit and was moving. No forwarding address.

AUNT JUNE. Those birds there? Sure they'll migrate. They're all done raising their babies. They'll be flying down to Mexico any week now.

BOY ROB. But then they fly back. I mean later. Right?

ROB'S MOTHER. I don't know where he found that album. *Sounds of a Southern Swamp.* He liked it here, but he missed Louisiana. He missed cane syrup and crawfish in the spring and fireflies and even humidity. When the fog would come in in July and you'd freeze to death, he couldn't believe it. I'd find that record on the turntable. He liked to play it late at night. I'm surprised he gave it up. He was possessive with his records. But I think he wanted you to know where he was from, and where you're from, too. Same with the tape of his show. A picture tells a thousand words, but you get a thousand pictures from somebody's voice.

ROB'S GRANDMOTHER *(reading)*. "Legacy. 1. A gift of property, especially personal property, by will. 2. Anything handed down from the past, as from an ancestor or predecessor."

MALE RADIO ANNOUNCER. Madame Butterfly, however, has not given up hope, and in response sings her famous aria, "*Un bel di*"—

ROB *(reading)*. "I fantasized his return constantly. I looked for him in crowds, in passing cars, at Giants games. I became a believer in omens and bargains. If I got straight A's in school, he'd come back. If I didn't spend any of my birthday money, he'd come back."

MALE RADIO ANNOUNCER. —describing in detail how Pinkerton will one day sail into the harbor, come up the hill—

BOY ROB *(reading)*. "Louisiana's major products are petroleum, natural gas, sugarcane, rice—"

ROB *(reading)*. "When the new phonebook came out every year, I checked for 'Guidry' and called up any new candidates I hadn't tried before, hoping he was still nearby."

WOMAN ON TELEPHONE. Sorry, darlin'. There's no Leonard here. I don't give out my name, but it sure ain't Leonard.

BOY ROB. Do you *know* a Leonard Guidry? Is he maybe in your family?

WOMAN ON TELEPHONE. In my family? Hmmm. Well, let's see. We got us a Leroy. You want him? Honey, you can have him, 'cause he's a mean son of a—

ROB *(reading)*. "My campaign was private, invisible to others, never revealed even to my mother. Ineffective charms were replaced by new ones. Every brown pelican I saw—Louisiana's state bird—brought his return a day closer. I began to think of the long stairway in our house as the Mississippi. The landing was St. Louis and the bottom step was Louisiana. I stepped on it twice, to show I hadn't forgotten him."

AUNT JUNE. Most migrating birds breed in the north, then go south for the winter. But brown pelicans are different. The ones we have here breed down in Mexico and the Channel Islands, then they fly *north*. Exactly the opposite of what most birds do.

BOY ROB. Are you sure?

ROB. I remember when you said that, it seemed a bad sign. I wanted a father who was like all the others.

AUNT JUNE. Of course you did.

ROB'S MOTHER, GRANDPARENTS, AUNTS *(singing)*.
　　Happy Birthday dear Robbie—

AUNT JESSICA. You got all the candles!

ROB'S GRANDFATHER. He always does.

ROB *(reading)*. "In fourth grade, we studied the myth of
　　Theseus, each student reading a paragraph from the book
　　out loud. Theseus doesn't know who his father is, but
　　knows the secret is buried under a huge stone. When
　　he's sixteen, he's strong enough to move it. Underneath
　　are sandals and a sword with the royal insignia of Ath-
　　ens. His father is King of Athens, and left these tokens
　　to identify himself. I felt myself flushing, felt sure all
　　eyes were on me. I couldn't find my voice to read. My
　　father, too, had left me tokens."

LENNY. The Beatles doing "Yesterday" for—

BOY ROB. —another satisfied customer here on the Ghost
　　Raising. Lenny here with you till one a.m.

LENNY. Next up, risking excommunication from the AM
　　airwaves—

ROB'S GRANDFATHER. I swear to God, if I hear that
　　tape one more time—

ROB'S GRANDMOTHER. Shhh! He'll hear you!

ROB *(reading)*. "Theseus immediately set off for Athens.
　　But no one knew where my father was. Just hoping he'd
　　come back wasn't enough. So I went searching. I did
　　this at night. I did it on the radio."

FEMALE RADIO ANNOUNCER. KNBR, San Francisco,
　　680.

MALE RADIO ANNOUNCER. Charlie Grant with you till
　　midnight—

FEMALE CALLER. I've never called a psychic before.

MALE RADIO ANNOUNCER. I'm sensing something quite vulnerable in your aura, Shana. I'm wondering if maybe you've suffered a setback, maybe something seemingly minor, perhaps a loss of some sort, something fairly recent, or perhaps in the past?

FEMALE CALLER. How could you know that? You're so amazing.

ROB *(reading)*. "My father had been a DJ. He might not have left the area. Long after my mother had fallen asleep, I'd be up in my room with the lights off and my headphones on. He could be anywhere on the dial."

MALE RADIO ANNOUNCER. —what it really means to live in Christ, to go to Him and ask Him to take your—

ROB *(reading)*. "He was Lenny Guidry, but he might be 'Leonard Goodrich' at a classical station, a name my mother had said he'd once used on the air. He could be 'Leo' or 'Len' or 'Lenny' playing top forty. 'LG' playing jazz. 'Leonardo' doing psychic readings."

MALE RADIO ANNOUNCER. Jeff in Oakland, your thoughts on the Raiders' kicking game.

ROB *(reading)*. "I liked hearing DJs start their shifts—the party-like banter, joking with the engineer. Station sign-offs, by contrast—"

MALE RADIO ANNOUNCER. In compliance with the Federal Communications Commission—

FEMALE RADIO ANNOUNCER. —will resume transmission at—

MALE RADIO ANNOUNCER. K217CR, ninety-two point four, Morgan Hill. K256AE eighty-nine point—

FEMALE RADIO ANNOUNCER. This concludes our—

MALE RADIO ANNOUNCER. —is now going off the air. *(Pause.)*

ROB *(reading)*. "Listening to the static where the signal had been was like witnessing a death. Sign-offs seemed to tell me my father was nowhere to be found. I tried not to hear them."

FEMALE RADIO ANNOUNCER. Jenny Smith, taking your calls about relationships, family, the holidays—

MALE RADIO ANNOUNCER. Are you tired of itching, burning feet? Coming up, Dr. Karl Engelmann—

FEMALE RADIO ANNOUNCER. *Ochocientos ochenta, la voz de San José-é-é-é-é!*

ROB *(reading)*. "Radio was a hundred-tongued cacophony. One of those voices, I felt certain, was his. All I had to do was find it."

(We hear the swamp sounds before, during and after the excerpt from LENNY's show.)

LENNY. So let's check in with the message machine.

MALE CALLER. Hi, Lenny. So anyway, today is what *would* have been our tenth anniversary, if you get my meaning, so I'd like you to send this out to my ex, kinda summing up the whole decade, a song called "Ninety-Six Tears," I forget who it was that—

MALE RADIO ANNOUNCER. —the post-game show with Rick and Ron.

FEMALE RADIO ANNOUNCER. Christy Russo with this news update—

MALE RADIO ANNOUNCER. El Lobo with you till five a.m.—

FEMALE RADIO ANNOUNCER. Carrie, playing all your country favorites—

MALE RADIO ANNOUNCER. The Reverend Bob Cuthbert—

FEMALE RADIO ANNOUNCER. Amy, Jim, Brett and the whole KCBS news team.

ROB *(reading)*. "Radio was an ocean of names. By sixth grade, I still hadn't heard his. I began losing faith, at least in the local stations. If he missed Louisiana so much, he'd probably gone back. I needed to pull in more-distant stations. That was when I started hanging out and asking questions at Ray's Electronics on 18th."

RAY. It's like this, chief. When the sun goes down, the radio waves go higher in the atmosphere without getting absorbed. They shoot up through the D level and get all the way to the F, maybe a hundred and fifty miles up.

ROB *(reading)*. "The place was dim as a cave and crammed with old equipment. Ray kept two ashtrays busy at a time, one at the phone and one on the counter, enveloping the shop in its own atmosphere composed of 2% oxygen and 98% cigarette smoke, the price of his otherwise free advice."

RAY. And then bam! They bounce off the F at an angle and come back, maybe a hundred, maybe a thousand, maybe a couple thousand miles from where they started. That's called skip. And skip, my friend, is your friend.

MALE RADIO ANNOUNCER. Wally Clark—

FEMALE RADIO ANNOUNCER. —and Paula Dinsmore—

MALE RADIO ANNOUNCER. —here with you for the radio swap meet. If you've got something to sell or trade—

FEMALE RADIO ANNOUNCER. —preferably not recently stolen—

RAY. Twilight's when you can pick up the little guys. At night, the big guns come out—fifty thousand kilowatts and up. Instead of out, they're aiming a lot of their signal up and counting on skip to really increase their range.

ROB *(reading)*. "I saved my money and bought a stereo tuner from Ray. While everyone else listened to the local stations, I loitered in the gaps in between, hoping for distant signals. I ventured east into the Central Valley: Mexican music, tubas pumping like steam engines, country western stations with weepy steel guitars, the farm report, ads for pesticides, preachers requesting donations to be sent to Redding or Fresno or Bakersfield. Sometimes, I'd pick up Eugene, Oregon, or KKOB in Albuquerque. It was thrilling to be able to search at such a distance."

ROB'S GRANDFATHER. What do you mean, no fluorescent lights?

BOY ROB. Ray says that's what's causing the buzzing on the radio.

ROB'S GRANDMOTHER. You need a new desk light anyway.

ROB'S GRANDFATHER. No I don't!

ROB'S GRANDMOTHER. Or you could wait till Robbie's asleep to use it.

ROB'S GRANDFATHER. What am I—Anne Frank in my own house? Next it'll be no loud foods. No raw carrots!

MALE RADIO ANNOUNCER. —and calling all the play-by-play, here's Frank Balasteri.

FEMALE RADIO ANNOUNCER. Sue Smith with the news—

MALE RADIO ANNOUNCER. —so pleased you're with us tonight and that you're part of our radio family of the air.

ROB *(reading)*. "No matter how distant, radio was much the same everywhere. Anyone could join the family of listeners. The out-of-state announcers were my great-uncles and second cousins, less familiar than the locals but still relatives."

FEMALE RADIO ANNOUNCER. KCWW, Tempe, Arizona, where the time is ten past midnight. Sally Winston spending the wee hours—

RAY. The sticker says twelve dollars. You got twelve dollars?

BOY ROB. No.

RAY. Then twelve dollars is just the "suggested retail price." How much you got to spend, my friend?

BOY ROB. Seven dollars.

RAY. Sold.

ROB *(reading)*. "I bought an old AM amp from Ray. He threw in some speaker wire for free and told me to tape it around my bedroom ceiling for an antenna. That night I pulled in Dallas, Texas. Then KTRH in Houston. I felt I was on my father's trail. Then—"

FEMALE RADIO ANNOUNCER. High tomorrow, ninety-one degrees, relative humidity about the same, so stay cool out there. Drink plenty of liquids and keep your radio tuned to the coolest place on the dial— KWKH, Shreveport.

ROB *(reading)*. "I'd found Louisiana. I could hardly believe it. It was foggy and frigid in San Francisco, but I could hear thunderstorms crackling along the line, scratching out the DJ's voice. They implied distance, dripping heat, little crossroad towns. The signal faded, fought back, faded again. I listened for hours. There was no mention of my father. Even so, I couldn't stop peering down on such a far-off, foreign place."

ROB'S GRANDMOTHER *(reading)*. "Camera obscura. A darkened box-like device in which images of external and often distant objects, admitted through an aperture, are exhibited in their natural colors."

ROB'S MOTHER. In Shreveport?

BOY ROB. Yeah.

ROB'S MOTHER. Hmmm. I doubt it. His family's down around Lafayette, in the Cajun part of the state. Or they used to be. I tried calling once, but his parents must have moved. I guess they could be in Shreveport. It's up north. Pretty different worlds, from what he said.

AUNT JESSICA. I think it was for your twelfth birthday. I'd seen it in a catalog of educational toys at school. And I knew right away it was meant for you.

AUNT JUNE. I remember I gave you birding binoculars that year—good ones. But when you opened up that shortwave radio kit, she'd trumped me. *She* was your favorite aunt.

AUNT JESSICA. Since it was a kit, I thought Nick could help you put it together. Another of my father-son, quality time get-togethers. Or that was the theory.

NICK. You gotta be kidding. Listen to this! "Locate now wires H and J, vigilantly having remove insulations previous to solder to E and F respectfully, kindly to consult the Figure 12." Can you believe that? Every sentence is like that! This translator oughta go build his own *electric chair*! And then *sit in it*!

ROB. Nick's not really all that mechanical, is he?

AUNT JESSICA. He's a P.E. teacher. I thought that was
    enough.

ROB'S MOTHER. It was as if you were building Franken-
    stein. Working at night, smoke from the soldering iron,
    attaching a speaker instead of a voice box. And then
    when you finished and the moment finally came for
    plugging it in, sending electricity through it, and we all
    heard that high static, like a baby's first cry—

ROB'S GRANDMOTHER. And then the first station.

ROB'S MOTHER. The creature's first words.

AUNT JUNE. Wasn't it cricket scores?

AUNT JESSICA. And even Nick smiled.

ROB'S GRANDMOTHER. The sound of Big Ben tolling,
    very low, and then—

MALE RADIO ANNOUNCER. This is the world service
    of the BBC.

ROB'S MOTHER. It was like watching a boat being
    launched. Everyone clapped.

ROB (reading). "They celebrated. I waited for them to
    leave. The shortwave was more than a new toy. My
    mother had a friend who'd moved to Paris to broadcast
    in English for Radio France. I'd wondered if my father
    might have done something similar. There was now no-
    where on earth that I couldn't search for him."

FEMALE RADIO ANNOUNCER. This is Sofia, Bulgaria
    calling.

MALE RADIO ANNOUNCER —broadcasting on the
    nineteen and twenty-five meter bands.

FEMALE RADIO ANNOUNCER. You're tuned to Radio
    Australia, the overseas—

MALE RADIO ANNOUNCER. —the English service of the Far East Broadcasting Company, transmitting from the Philippines on fifteen four four five, seventeen—

ROB *(reading)*. "I began writing to stations, sending reception reports in exchange for QSL cards—verifications sent by stations, collected by shortwave listeners. A month later, the mail began arriving. Along with the QSL might be a decal, a schedule, a magazine, a pennant, or all of the above. I began getting more mail than my mother got. Some of it kept coming for years. I always checked the station manager's signature on the QSL, waiting to see the name 'Leonard Guidry.'"

ROB'S GRANDMOTHER. What is it, Robbie?

BOY ROB. Another Christmas card. From Radio Norway. Look.

ROB'S GRANDFATHER. My own *brother* hasn't sent me a card in twenty years—and you get one from Radio Norway!

ROB *(reading)*. "I met new kids in middle school. I made new friends. But my radio world was private. It became more public, however, the day I saw a baby monitor at a garage sale. I stood and stared at it for five minutes, not knowing why. Then, in a flash, I saw what it could do. I bought it for a dollar, plugged the speaker in near my mother's bed, and took the microphone into my room."

ROB'S MOTHER. Remember? Of course I remember. I wrote a poem about it, called "Sign On."

BOY ROB. It's seven-thirteen on this sunny Saturday morning in San Francisco, except that in the time it took to say that it's now actually seven-thirteen and fifteen seconds, seven-thirteen and twenty seconds, twenty-five seconds, thirty seconds, anyway, you're tuned to

K-ROB, so don't touch that dial, which you can't anyway 'cause it's set to just this one frequency—

ROB'S MOTHER. The programming content was a little
thin, but the concept was fabulous.

BOY ROB. Over to you Rob, in Traffic-copter Two.
How's it look?

ROB'S GRANDMOTHER. And then, remember? He'd use
the electric pencil sharpener, to sound like the helicopter
engine.

ROB'S MOTHER. Till every pencil in the house was half
an inch long.

BOY ROB. "There's no traffic coming in on the Golden
Gate, Ed. Not a single car. Same with the Richmond and
the Bay Bridge." "What is this, Rob, some kind of joke?
It's Monday." "It's not *my* fault, Ed. There's *just no
cars*!" "This is too weird! Something's wrong. Mabel—
start the civil defense siren!"

ROB'S MOTHER. And you'd gotten a real siren somewhere.

ROB. In a junk shop.

ROB'S MOTHER. Good old Mabel and Ed. I miss
K-ROB. What was next?

ROB. There was KOP.

BOY ROB *(reading)*. "It was a rotten business, detective
work, and at the moment business was rotten. He'd quit
the racket once and sworn he'd never come back. But
here he was—his name on the door and his feet on the
desk."

ROB'S GRANDMOTHER. "KOP—your station for cops
and robbers." Right in our bedroom. And then the siren.
Which was really quite loud, I have to admit. And that
first time, when you took us by surprise—

ROB. And Grandpa thought it was an earthquake, the Big One—

ROB'S MOTHER. And then the heart palpitations and the emergency room.

ROB'S GRANDMOTHER. He was fine. And Robbie didn't mean to scare him.

AUNT JUNE. Sure. You slept over at my place. And in the morning, out of nowhere I heard this duck screeching in my ear.

BOY ROB. "Ninety-one point five, KWAK, quack radio, all birds, all the time. And here's Rob, with the morning bird report." "Thanks, Joe. We've got heavy pelican traffic northbound, from Half Moon Bay all the way—"

ROB *(reading)*. "Had my father made up his own stations, too? What had I inherited from him? I liked Cajun music, but was hopeless at playing instruments. I would take the few pictures of him we had, go into the bathroom, lock the door, and compare our noses in the mirror, then our eyes, chins, left profiles, right profiles."

RAY. The sound's lousy? What do you expect? It's a baby monitor. You got it for a buck, my friend. With a buck you get peanuts, not chicken Kiev.

ROB *(reading)*. "So Ray sold me a public address amp, a mike, and a twenty-watt speaker."

AUNT JESSICA. For one of your birthdays I bought you that CD with all the sound effects, remember? Screams, church bells, squealing tires—

BOY ROB. It's time now, listeners, for radio aerobics. Let's begin with a few easy warm-ups. Bring your left arm around behind your back as far as you can. *(Sound of bones cracking.)* Good. Now *stretch* those legs wide apart. *(Sound of bones cracking.)*

AUNT JESSICA. You really got a lot of use out of the bone-cracking track.

ROB'S GRANDMOTHER. What I liked best were the stories you'd do completely out of sounds. They were like dreams. You must have had a turntable and a tape player and a CD player. You'd have the swamp sounds going for a while all alone, then on top of that you'd put accordion music, real soft—

ROB *(reading)*. "I'd imagine us in a cabin, somewhere in Louisiana. It was night and we were rocking in the dark, unable to see each other, him playing his accordion—"

ROB'S GRANDMOTHER. Then there might be a scream. Or footsteps. Then suddenly we'd be in London. You'd taped Big Ben off your shortwave. We'd hear it tolling, over and over.

ROB *(reading)*. "All this time, I was staying up half the night listening to shortwave. Still looking for him."

AUNT JUNE. Or storms can blow birds way off course. They're called vagrants. They might end up on the wrong side of the continent, or on the wrong continent altogether. Then, next season, they get back on track.

ROB *(reading)*. "Toward the end of eighth grade, instead of losing hope, I felt surer than ever that the meeting with my father was approaching. I was about to turn thirteen, a year behind my classmates, the result of skipping second grade. That year my birthday fell on the last day of school. I knew from my mother that birthdays were important to him. His own family had given him a huge party for his thirteenth, where they'd given him his first accordion. I knew that my father was aware of my birthdate. And I knew that thoughts, like radio waves, skip thousands of miles. I knew he was thinking about

me and would want to be a part of my gates-of-adult-
hood birthday. Twice I'd caught my mother talking very
softly on the phone lately. He'd find out about graduation and would want to be there for that momentous
event as well. About that time, the bottom stair suddenly
began squeaking. The Louisiana stair."

ROB'S MOTHER. We'd decided to celebrate your birthday after the graduation ceremony, which started at six—

ROB'S GRANDFATHER. —and lasted about fourteen hours.
The orchestra, the chorus, the school board, the speeches.

ROB *(reading)*. "It didn't seem long or slow to me. When I
marched down the aisle, looking straight ahead as they'd
taught us, I could feel his eyes on my back, and I
smiled. A second skin of sweat covered me. When I finally reached the stage and turned, I spotted my family
near the front. The auditorium was deep and packed, a
confetti of faces, those in the rear third shadowed by the
balcony."

ROB'S MOTHER. You were so lost, you didn't notice
when they called your name for the scholarship award.

ROB *(reading)*. "We got our diplomas. Amazingly, they'd
spelled 'Radkovitz' correctly. Miracles were in the air.
Row by row, we filed back down and outside to the
courtyard. By the time I arrived, it was mobbed. I
squeezed onto a bench and stood—not to find my family, but so my father could find me. I waved my arms
discreetly, at no one in particular. I thought to myself—"

BOY ROB. You're crazy. He's not here. Don't wave your
arms.

ROB *(reading)*. "Then in my mind other voices answered
back."

RAY. You know, my friend, radio men kinda have a sixth sense, between themselves. I had two other radio buddies in Korea—

MALE RADIO ANNOUNCER. —as he reminds us in Second Corinthians, "For we walk by faith, not by sight."

ROB *(reading)*. "My family found me and took pictures. My eyes were everywhere but on the camera. I made the excuse of looking for friends and circulated through the crowd, waiting to be noticed. People began leaving. I told myself that I hadn't really thought he'd come, even though I knew this was false. Then it hit me. Maybe he hadn't told my mother. Maybe his appearance would be a surprise. Maybe he didn't know it was graduation night, so instead of at school, he'd be waiting at the house, after our dinner at a restaurant."

MALE RADIO ANNOUNCER. —part of our radio family of the air.

ROB *(reading)*. "This failed to happen also. At home, I turned the cake and presents into a funeral. They all knew that something was wrong, inquired gently, saw I couldn't tell them, and tried to make the best of the evening. I headed upstairs. I flipped on the radio. It was on AM, far down in the six hundreds. I punched the seek button. The tuner jumped to 680."

MALE RADIO ANNOUNCER. —mowed down the Giants, thirteen strikeouts in—

ROB *(reading)*. "I punched it again."

FEMALE RADIO ANNOUNCER. —traffic and weather every ten minutes.

ROB *(reading)*. "Again. Harder."

MALE RADIO ANNOUNCER. —car insurance rates you can live with.

ROB *(reading)*. "Over—"

FEMALE RADIO ANNOUNCER. *Por la comida mas sabrosa de*—

MALE RADIO ANNOUNCER. —reports of scattered gunfire—"

ROB *(reading)*. "—and over—"

FEMALE RADIO ANNOUNCER. —will steam-clean all your carpets—

ROB *(reading)*. "—and over—"

MALE RADIO ANNOUNCER. On Wall Street, the Dow was up twenty-nine—

ROB *(reading)*. "—and over—"

FEMALE RADIO ANNOUNCER. —two free tickets to give away to the fifth caller.

ROB *(reading)*. "—until I'd punched it—*"*

MALE RADIO ANNOUNCER. —an all-you-can-eat breakfast sponsored—

ROB *(reading)*. "—to the end of the dial.*"*

FEMALE RADIO ANNOUNCER. Easy listening one-oh-seven point—

MALE RADIO ANNOUNCER. The Beach Boys doing "Good Vibrations."

ROB *(reading)*. "Then I slammed my fist down on the radio. I grabbed the cord and yanked the plug out of the socket. The dial lost its light. I stared at it in triumph. And straight to its face I yelled out my birthday wish."

BOY ROB. I hope I never meet him!

ROB *(reading)*. "Then—"

BOY ROB. And I'm through with radios!

END OF ACT ONE

ACT TWO

(We hear the swamp sounds before, during and after LENNY's excerpt.)

FEMALE CALLER. Hey, Lenny. Take me back to the thirties, OK? You know, people talk about "the music of the spheres," the universe's music, but it ain't what people think. It ain't harps strumming and prissy little hymns. I got news for people. 'Cause the music of the spheres—man, it's Big Band music.

LENNY. I'm with you. So here's a number by Count Basie himself, one of his most famous, "One O'clock Jump," recorded back in 1937 at—

ENGLISH TEACHER. I don't believe this. Can't anyone in the class—I'll read it one last time. "She was wearing a sombrero *on her head* which came from Mexico." What's wrong with that sentence?

FEMALE STUDENT *(pause)*. It really came from Guatemala?

ROB. Hey, Zad, what about this? I put in a legal disclaimer. "The opinions expressed about this school in the following work are not necessarily the author's, even though it's an autobiography."

ZAD. Cute, Rob.

COACH. C'mon, men—cut the moaning and sighing! Chin-ups are easy! Give it all you've got! Show me a hundred and ten, a hundred and twenty percent! Winkler! How many was that?

MALE STUDENT. Three.

COACH. Was that giving a hundred and twenty percent?

MALE STUDENT. Actually, you can't really, I'm like taking pre-calculus, but we studied percentages back in fourth grade, and it's not like actually possible to give *more than* a hundred—

COACH. You're not in math class—you're in the gym! And in the gym it's possible! Now get back up there and pull!

ENGLISH TEACHER. "—wearing a sombrero *on her head which came from Mexico*." Did her *head* come from Mexico? Did she buy it for five pesos in the market? Did you all buy yours at the same stall?

DEAN. I've been a dean here a good long time, and believe me you're not the first. We run into this every few years. A particular class comes in and thinks they can break all the rules. They want four strikes before they strike out. Special treatment. Just throw the rule book out the window. But I'm the ref around here. And let me tell you—

ROB *(reading)*. "I was nervous about high school. My three best friends had taken the private school exit. Jefferson looked like a battleship: huge, gray, a scarred survivor of a thousand vandal attacks. Two other unknown middle schools converged here, pouring strangers into the halls. I'd never gone to a school with security guards before. They lent the cafeteria that prison ambience so conducive to loss of appetite. After two days I begged my mother to let me home-school, but she—"

MRS. DRUCKENMULLER. A first-year reporter, as we know, is called a "cub." Let's welcome our three new cub reporters—Zad, Gloria and Rob.

FEMALE STUDENT. The three bears.

MALE STUDENT. Here cubbie cubbie cubbie!

ZAD. Mrs. Druckenmuller?

MRS. DRUCKENMULLER. Yes, Zad.

ZAD. What I don't get is why we're the Jefferson Jets. I mean Thomas Jefferson believed in a country of small farmers, right? Which doesn't exactly go with jet planes.

MRS. DRUCKENMULLER. Well, I suppose—

MALE STUDENT. What do you want—the Hicks?

FEMALE STUDENT. The Tillers?

MALE STUDENT. Who cares what Jefferson thought? It's all about headlines on the sports page. "Jets Strafe Pirates." "Jets Bomb Palo Alto Back to Stone Age." "Jets Flush Toilet Over—"

MRS. DRUCKENMULLER. Thank you, Tony.

ROB'S MOTHER. You remember that day, Rob? Here's the page. "March 4th. Bees among the almond blossoms, going door to door to door. Wings thrumming, stirring the scents in the air, mixing spring into winter." Just images and ideas. At least that's what I use mine for. Not finished poems, but materials. Wood stacked next to a building site.

ROB *(reading)*. "I'd put my shortwave in the attic that summer. Writing had replaced radio. I began keeping a journal, like my mother. We took sketching trips, recording scenes in words: the Sonoma vineyards, Muir Woods, Skid Row. She let me sit in on her writing group—"

FEMALE WRITER. This is a little haiku I've been polishing for a couple of months, actually since last summer when I went to the Japanese tea garden. Or was it spring? The rhododendrons were in bloom, I recall. Quite lovely. Anyway, I'd be especially grateful for Rob's reaction, as the youngest member of the group. Because I think it's a subject that's really more likely to resonate with a—

MALE WRITER. A haiku has seventeen syllables, Marjorie. You've already used up a hundred and ninety.

ROB *(reading)*. "My mother suggested I join the school paper. The *Jefferson Jetstream* bore little resemblance to the Washington *Post* in *All the President's Men*. The editorials had to be approved by the entire administration and dealt with such hard-hitting issues as—"

FEMALE STUDENT *(reading)*. "—even though they may be in a hurry, students must stop and realize that running, bumping, and even shoving each other has made our hallways nearly as dangerous as the freeways. We believe that it's time—

ROB. Hey, Zad—how old is Mrs. Druckenmuller anyway?

ZAD. I think she was here when the Indians crossed the land bridge from Asia, *Zad responded informatively.*

MRS. DRUCKENMULLER. Always try to spice up your stories with interesting verbs. Never use "said." I want you all to see what a fine job Jennifer did in her interview with the vice principal. *(Reading.)* "'I've always enjoyed sports,' *he commented.* 'Before serving as vice principal, I coached the Jets' football and wrestling teams,' *he added thoughtfully.*" Now that's some fine, lively reporting.

ROB *(reading)*. "October 8th. Driving back from Sierras, we parked to watch a huge flock of swirling blackbirds. Flock bends in half like blanket being folded and unfolded by invisible hands. Morphs in air like a living screen-saver. Sudden movements executed by all members simultaneously: a marching band without a drum major."

ROB'S GRANDFATHER. Such a waste. Ridiculous! There was immigration, drug laws, AIDS—

ROB'S GRANDMOTHER. —the environment, First Amendment issues with the Internet. So many topics a school paper ought to be tackling.

ROB *(reading)*. "Like the *Jetstream*, high school in general wasn't what I'd expected. I'd imagined it as just a step below Stanford and Berkeley. Instead, it turned out to be run largely by former P.E. coaches, whose motivational and crowd-control skills apparently qualified them to become administrators. Order was the order of the day, not education. We were still being handed pre-fab worksheets from teacher guides. I had no inspiring teachers my first year. In class, Habit Bingo was a popular student pastime."

FEMALE STUDENT *(whispering throughout scene)*. See how she keeps touching her hair?

ROB. Yeah.

FEMALE STUDENT. So every time she does, you get to fill in that square. Same with running her tongue over her front teeth, or staring at the Nathaniel Hawthorne poster.

ROB. What's that about, anyway?

FEMALE STUDENT. Maybe she's got the hots for him. He's been dead for like hundreds of years, right?

ROB. Right.

FEMALE STUDENT. She must have given up on the dating scene. Totally. Now look at my card. If she says the word "glean"—

ENGLISH TEACHER. *Silas Marner*, chapter seven. Who can tell me what you gleaned from—

FEMALE STUDENT. Bingo!

ROB *(reading)*. "Mrs. Druckenmuller put great emphasis on the traditions of journalism, such as typing the number thirty at the bottom of a story, ancient reporter code for 'the end.'"

ZAD. She'd actually mark you off if you didn't. Remember? But I was so sick of our stupid, limp carrot of a newspaper that I typed a twenty-nine at the bottom. Which you saw. And the elevator started heading down.

ROB. Twenty-eight.

ZAD. Twenty-seven.

ROB. Twenty-five and a half.

ZAD. Eleven.

ROB. We were puny freshmen. Pretty amazing, really. This was like storming the bastille. Open revolt. Druckenmuller gave us that lecture.

ZAD. You said they were typos.

ROB. Then we switched to Roman numerals.

ZAD. Then you thought up the equations that equaled thirty.

ROB. Two X plus five, times eighty over two—

ZAD. —minus fourteen squared, divided by three—

ROB. It was the first time I'd gotten less than an "A" in behavior.

ZAD. Late bloomer.

ROB *(reading)*. "By spring of freshman year, Zad and I had had enough. We started our own underground paper, called the *Jefferson Other*. We did reviews of movies and music."

ZAD. And teachers. Man, we were brutal.

ROB. They deserved it.

ZAD. Then Penelope joined and did the Fall Anti-Fashion Report. Then the story on minimum wage.

ROB. Real news that was relevant to students.

ZAD. Then, for Jefferson's fiftieth anniversary, remember, you blew their heads off with that story on Thomas Jefferson's half-black children.

ROB'S GRANDFATHER. Give 'em hell, Robbie! That's my boy.

ROB *(reading)*. "That issue got us all called into the dean's."

ZAD. Just possibly because Penelope doctored his photo and gave him a pig's snout.

PENELOPE. It was just a little one.

ROB'S MOTHER. My favorite? Well, I was a huge "Ann Philanders" fan, of course.

PENELOPE *(reading)*. "Dear Confused Sophomore: I've gone through the entire Bible—and guess what? There's absolutely *nothing* prohibiting sex with a computer science teacher. So relax and enjoy. He sounds like a wonderful man. If it doesn't work out, maybe you'd be kind enough to give him my—"

ZAD. And then there was the tabloid issue, with the front page done just like *The National Enquirer*.

ROB. "DNA Tests Reveal Entire Cafeteria Staff From Distant Galaxy."

ZAD. Not all that far-fetched, really.

PENELOPE. Off to the dean's again.

DEAN. I suppose that you all know how to read.

ROB. Fairly obvious.

DEAN. You can cut the flippancy right there. I want you to do me a little reading aloud. Start with that paragraph, from the California Education Code. The section on student publications.

ROB. It was sort of a badge of honor, being called in to the dean's office.

ZAD. We sure got ourselves a big badge collection.

ROB *(reading)*. "One night, through the door that connected our two halves of the house, I heard my mother and grandparents—"

ROB'S GRANDFATHER. —at Lenny. And what's wrong with him channeling it into that? He's running an underground paper, not stealing cars. He's found himself some fine substitutes to attack. Who was out with the ropes and crowbars, tearing down the statues of Lenin all over Europe? Men who hate their fathers, that's who.

ROB *(reading)*. "The hairs on my head straightened. I knew he was right. But this didn't lead me to sound the retreat. It was something else entirely that caused that."

ROB'S MOTHER. "On your hands,
  sap stains dark as birthmarks,
  potent as smelling salts:
  The scent of new rooms."

ROB *(reading)*. "When my mother finally couldn't stand our old kitchen cabinets another minute, she had a carpenter put in new ones. The cabinet job led to others. He always read a book while he ate lunch in his truck. My mother noticed this and they started talking books. His name was Andrew. Then he became Andy."

ROB'S MOTHER. "On my fingertips:
  minced garlic, shallots,

shrimp, red pepper,
a scale model of dinner—"

ZAD. Did you ever notice how everyone picked boyfriends
or girlfriends from the other middle schools. It was like
we were tired of the same old faces.

ROB. Mick and Christa.

ZAD. Penelope and Sean.

ROB. The lure of the exotic.

ZAD. Like Mr. Wirtz was saying in biology. It's exogamy.

ROB'S GRANDMOTHER *(reading)*. "Exogamy: Marrying
outside one's family, tribe, or social unit."

ROB *(reading)*. "I saw this in my mother as well. Andy
could build things, unlike anyone else in my family. He
was quieter than us. I think we were all impressed by
someone who didn't feel the need to constantly tell the
world everything he was thinking. He was blond, as
none of us were. And he liked to read fantasy."

ANDY *(reading)*. "—had vowed never to submit to the ty-
rannical rule of Gunthor, whose armies, captained by his
half-brother Ogrit, had spread terror throughout Kalan-
dria, just as the seer Simso had predicted before he'd
been slain by Gunthor's uncle, Heffelvorp."

ROB *(reading)*. "—a genre utterly unrepresented on our
many bookshelves."

PENELOPE. "Dear Ann Philanders: There's a guy I like
whom I'll call Pope Julius II (not his real name). I've
tried every line in *Scoring for Dummies*, *Reproduction
for Dummies*, and *Matrimony for Dummies* but nothing
has worked. How can I hook him?" "Dear Desperate: It
seems pretty clear that you just aren't his taste in bait.
Take the hint. And if you wouldn't mind passing him
my number and photo—"

ROB *(reading)*. "My mother had had boyfriends over the years, but nothing long-lasting or serious, at least as far as I knew. Andy was different. He came to dinners with my grandparents, then backpacking in the Sierras with us that summer. We got call waiting—ostensibly for me, since my friends called a lot—but really for my mother."

ROB'S MOTHER. Hey—we're gonna go for a walk.

ROB *(reading)*. "He brought over a cribbage board he'd made and taught my mother to play. To his credit, he never forced the game, or anything else, on me. He was pleasant, patient, easy to be around. But something in me resisted him."

ROB'S MOTHER. Maybe we'll get some ice cream.

ROB *(reading)*. "We. Pronoun. Plural. Specifically, Rob and Rose Radkovitz."

ANDY. You want to come along, Rob?

ROB *(reading)*. "Somehow the definition had changed. My mother and I shared interests to an unusual degree, almost always ate dinner together, almost always looked forward to it. In a way, we were like spouses. And in a way, I began feeling I was being divorced."

ROB'S MOTHER. Robbie—did you hear? June had the baby! A girl!

ROB. Hey, that's great. And I have something, too—an overdue history paper.

AUNT JESSICA. Come to the hospital with us, Rob. She's so gorgeous! Nick's coming over right after work. I want him to see. He hasn't ruled out adoption, but he wants some time. So I bought him a hamster. To get him used to taking care of something. After that, I thought maybe a kitten.

ROB'S GRANDMOTHER. A hamster?

AUNT JESSICA. Is that moving too fast?

ROB'S GRANDFATHER. I think you better back up. Maybe a rock collection. Coins. Something that doesn't eat.

ROB *(reading)*. "I knew I should have been overjoyed for Aunt June. She'd waited so long, first to find a husband, then to have a baby. Just as my mother had waited so long—"

ZAD. The exact same with my mom last year.

ROB. And whenever she's with him, they're always laughing. It's weird.

ZAD. It's a stage they go through.

ROB. What's to laugh about when you're doing a zillion dishes?

ZAD. Or hiking up some monster trail in the sun?

ROB. Last night they went to this lecture by some guy who'd been tortured in Argentina.

ZAD. Probably laughed their heads off.

SPANISH TV ACTRESS. *Nunca te voy a dar la foto. Nunca!*

ROB *(reading)*. "Andy was trying to learn Spanish, with my mother's help. His accent was hopeless. Vocabulary was also a problem. When we all went to a Mexican restaurant—"

ANDY. What's she laughing about? I asked her to put it in a doggie bag, right? *Un saco de perro.*

ROB'S MOTHER. Sweetie. You were trying your best. It's just dangerous, translating literally.

ANDY. So what did I say?

ROB'S MOTHER. You don't want to know.

ANDY. Actually, I do.

ROB'S MOTHER. Well, you—you asked her to put the food in a—in a—in a dog's scrotum.

ROB *(reading)*. "I laughed at him, too loudly I knew. He laughed at himself. My mother laughed with the waitress till she cried."

ZAD. In a dog's *scrotum*? And they're still together?

PENELOPE. Then it's serious. That's definitely one of the ten warning signs. I read it in Ann Philanders.

ROB *(reading)*. "They took me to things they thought would interest me. I was a mannequin in the car, a deaf-mute when we got there, a vanishing spirit when we returned. I knew I was being childish and churlish, but I couldn't stop myself. I was in a riptide, and couldn't swim out of it. Then one night my mother tried the direct approach. I was listening to music in the living room, in the dark. She turned it down, very slowly. Then she sat beside me. Then she said—"

ROB'S MOTHER. Tell me everything you're afraid of.

ROB *(reading)*. "I turned my face away. She put her arms around me like a life preserver. She held me, rocking slightly. We stayed that way for a solid hour. Then I started talking. The big issues first, then things like who sat where at the dinner table, then little things, like his yogurts filling up the fridge door. I talked until I couldn't find anything else to bring up. I felt drained. And then we slept, thirteen hours in my case. The next day, Andy was over for dinner. I sat at my old place at the table.

PENELOPE *(reading)*. "Dear Ann Philanders: The new guy my mom is going out with, who I'll call Krevkov, son of Borf (not his real name)—"

ROB *(reading)*. A month after that, I asked him to teach me how to play cribbage."

ROB'S GRANDMOTHER. You knew from making the bed together?

ROB'S MOTHER. You see how sensitive the other person is to your movements. If you communicate well without words. How much or little detail matters—smoothing out wrinkles, folding back the bedspread. For us, it was always this lovely duet. It's a tango, without touching.

ROB'S GRANDMOTHER. Your father's never made the bed in fifty-seven years.

ROB'S GRANDFATHER. Sorry, but the back doctor told me, "No tangos."

SPANISH TV ACTRESS. *Siempre recuerda.*

ANDY. Always—

ROB'S MOTHER. —remember—

SPANISH TV ACTRESS. *Te adoro.*

ANDY. I adore you.

SPANISH TV ACTRESS. *Te adoro.*

ROB'S MOTHER. I adore you.

ANDY. I adore you.

ROB'S MOTHER. Are you translating, or telling me something.

ANDY. Telling you something. For extra credit.

ROB *(reading)*. "My mother and Andy got married in Golden Gate Park. She kept her maiden name, for my sake, I think. Andy, his furniture, his large dog Marco, his yoga exercises, his talk radio stations, his chili recipe, his long baths, etc., entered our two-bedroom, one-bathroom home. It was like trying to squeeze—"

ROB. What do you think of the sign?

ROB'S MOTHER. "Mother of All Garage Sales." Great. But now it's time to live up to it. I'm getting rid of four whole boxes of books. You've got a bunch you haven't

read in years, up here and downstairs, that really ought
to—

ROB. I already went through all my books.

ROB'S MOTHER. And?

ROB. And—I'm selling those.

ROB'S MOTHER. *Five books?* Rob, honey, come on. Let's
look through them together. Look, right here. *Our Forest
Friends.* From preschool days. Do you still need that?

ROB. I might. You never know.

ZAD. He took you on Lombard? The steepest street in
freaking North America?

ROB. I swear that's one reason she got married, so she
wouldn't have to teach me to drive. So after Lombard—
you should try it, it's fun—we're on Van Ness and he
says how you have to learn to tune out distractions. So
he turns on the radio to a talk station.

FEMALE RADIO ANNOUNCER. —because the self-ap-
pointed liberal, humanist high priests who probably *are*
descended from monkeys—

ROB. And then he's got a boombox running on batteries in
the back seat, and he puts in a gospel tape—loud.

MALE RADIO ANNOUNCER. And that's why we praise
Him in the morning! Not just Sunday morning, but every morning, when the light rises in the east!

FEMALE RADIO ANNOUNCER. Fluoride in the water,
Darwinism in the schools—

ROB. Then he whips out a harmonica and starts honking
away on *that*, and I'm completely cracking up, trying to
stay in my lane—

ZAD. Maybe I'll get my mother to hire him.

ROB *(reading)*. "August 23rd. Andy's entrance: house
molts, new plumage. Different couch and coffee table.

New knick-knacks on my mother's bookshelf unattached to any memories of mine. Beat him at cribbage last night. His chili not bad."

ANDY. Seconds anyone?

ROB. For me, actually. Thanks.

ANDY. And can I put that in a dog's scrotum for you?

ROB. *Gracias.*

ANDY. *De nada.*

ROB *(reading).* "Sophomore year passed. In my junior year, I began learning some yoga from Andy—breathing exercises, simple positions. You're supposed to clear your mind of thoughts, but one night I was in a very restful position called the fallen leaf, while my mother graded papers and Andy was brushing the dog, and suddenly the thought struck me out of nowhere: My real father wasn't coming back. And then: And I don't really mind. I felt muscles, bones, joints, ligaments all go utterly slack. I felt like a marionette who'd been laid on the floor. I closed my eyes. To me, this felt like Nirvana, the state yoga masters spend lifetimes searching for."

1st BASEBALL ANNOUNCER. —tonight's Giants payoff inning, in which players bat for you, the fans. Who's our first lucky listener?

2nd BASEBALL ANNOUNCER. Let's see here. Jesus—

ROB & ANDY. Hay-ZOOSE!

1st BASEBALL ANNOUNCER. —MAN-u-el.

ROB & ANDY. Man-WELL!

ROB *(reading).* "Andy's arrival had brought this about. He was a person of regular habits. He was up whistling in the kitchen every morning, walked the dog every night, took a long bath every Friday. He'd been living with us a year, and in the picture for two before. He felt reliable and permanent. I could sight down his and my mother's life as I could down one of those straight Central Valley roads. Lenny was nowhere in that picture."

ROB'S GRANDPARENTS. And look at him blow!

ROB *(reading)*. "It was as if that whole issue had snapped shut, like a box. I heard the click of the clasp in that moment on the floor, and suddenly I knew that I could put that box up in the attic and stop looking at it. Which is exactly what I did in my mind."

ANDY. Then very slowly lean forward and just rest your forehead on the floor.

ROB *(reading)*. "I was still in the fallen leaf. Eyes closed, I imagined myself getting a cardboard box and putting inside it my photos of Lenny, the "Ghost Raising" tape, the sound-effects record, my little toy accordion, all my Louisiana school reports. I taped it shut. Then I pictured getting the ladder from the back porch, hauled it up the stairs, climbed up it, opened the trapdoor, pulled the light-chain, and crawled into the attic with the box. I mentally walked into the corner and set the box down next to the trunk. I stepped back and stared at it. Then, in real life, I opened my eyes. I stood up and collected myself. Then I did everything I'd just imagined."

(We hear the swamp sounds before, during and after LENNY's excerpt.)

MALE CALLER. Yeah, Lenny, would you play "Bésame Mucho" by Trio Los Panchos. I don't really want to discuss it. Thanks.

LENNY. Hey, I'm not here to pry. You want "Bésame Mucho"? Fine by me. *Lo que sea*, like my old lady used

to say. That's Spanish for "whatever." So without fur-
ther ado—

NEVA. So are you going to write about me?

ROB. Neva, c'mon. We're not supposed to tell McCarthy
everything. Remember?

MR. McCARTHY. Do you notice, class, that every burp
and sneeze isn't there. Writers pick and choose. Which I
hope you're doing, too. *Nothing over a thousand pages,
please.*

ROB. Am I in yours?

NEVA. You've got a few numbers after your name in the
index.

ZAD. It's unbelievable. Check out the names.

ROB. Radio Chaos International.

ZAD. Radio Garbanzo.

ROB. KMUD.

ZAD. Radio Free Texas.

ROB. The Voice of Laryngitis.

ZAD. The Voice of Stench.

ROB. *The Voice of Stench?*

ZAD. Now *that* is cool. We gotta hear that one.

ROB *(reading)*. "Zad had read an article in the *Chronicle*
about pirate radio stations. We'd given up on the underground paper a year before and were feeling the hole.
When I'd put the box of Lenny's stuff in the attic, I'd
passed by my shortwave. I now realized I could give up
boycotting radio. I wouldn't be searching for him or imi-
tating him. I'd be listening just because I wanted to. I
went back up and hauled it down. Finding pirate stations
turned out to be harder than reading about them. They
change frequencies, broadcast irregularly, get shut down.

The only one I found at first was giving a three-hour rant about the FCC that frankly—"

MALE RADIO ANNOUNCER. So how, you're wondering, did the FCC find him broadcasting from his houseboat some place in Minnesota. I mean there's ten thousand lakes in Minnesota, right? That's what it says on the license plate, anyway. Or is that Wisconsin? "The Show Me State." Hold on. That's Missouri. "Land of Lincoln." That's either Indiana or the other one—Illinois.

ZAD. Two thoughts. Choosing our own station name would be fun. And we can do better than this guy.

ROB. All I knew is that you were new and your name was Neva.

NEVA. And I didn't know anything about you. I'd just moved here. I couldn't believe school started in early August, or that August could be as cold as winter in Chicago. I remember seeing you that first day in English and you were reading some electronics magazine. And from that one detail I assumed you were a nerd and crossed you off my list. For three days, anyway.

ROB *(reading)*. "Zad and I pooled our money and bought a 3 watt FM transmitter from Ray. He threw in a used mixing board for fifty dollars and helped us make a quarter-wave antenna out of some scrounged tubing. Zad and I attached it to the pitched roof above my bedroom in a mere three hours and without attracting more than eight or so spectators waiting to see us plunge to our deaths, one of whom was filming us. That night we did a thirty-second test broadcast after midnight, me listening and recording in the living room while Zad was in my bedroom."

ZAD. This is KPOW, Ka-pow, your anarchist alternative, signing on and signing off. It's been great, and you've been a terrific audience.

ROB. It worked! I could hear it!

ZAD. Rewind the tape!

ROB *(reading)*. "September 10th. She's a river: long limbs, long black hair. Mystery of her source: the Midwest, unknown to me. Plays flute, bubbling source of rivers of music. She's read even more books than I have. Contemplating touching her, like a bather standing on a rock, afraid to jump in."

ZAD. —as we listen to this incredible skit from the very first Monty Python record, which is incredibly rare, and has this—

NEVA. —because people don't want to deal with homelessness anymore. They're tired of the issue. For them, it's like some TV show on endless reruns—

ROB *(reading)*. "Now we needed something worth broadcasting. Zad picked comedy, a pirate radio staple. Neva interviewed neighborhood characters and covered politics, which endeared her to my grandfather. I did poetry. For our sign-on, we used a recording of an explosion from my old sound-effects CD. At sign-off, we taped the song "We'll Meet Again" off the video of *Dr. Strangelove*, which comes on at the end of the movie when all the nuclear bombs are going off."

NEVA. Exactly. Radio by the neighborhood, for the neighborhood. So you were saying that you worked in the shipyards during World War Two. That must have been quite an experience.

OLD WOMAN. What's that?

NEVA *(as to someone hard of hearing). Your working in the shipyards.*

OLD WOMAN. Who?

NEVA. *You. Remember, you were telling me?*

OLD WOMAN. I said that?

NEVA. *Yesterday, when we were talking.*

OLD WOMAN. Yesterday… But I've never seen you before.

ZAD. Not quite ready for prime-time pirate radio. And by the way, the signal was pathetic.

AUNT JUNE. Sorry, Robbie. Couldn't hear a thing. I had it tuned right where you said.

ROB *(reading).* "On the one hand, we didn't have to worry about the FCC. On the other hand, no one was hearing us. We passed the collection plate among the pirate crew, went back to Ray, and bought a limiter, which was supposed to increase our range to several miles. Andy and I went out driving to see where we—"

ROB'S GRANDFATHER. It was the biggest general strike in American history.

ANDY. Hey, there it is! It's Gramps on the air! Check the trip meter.

ROB. Four point two miles.

NEVA. And you still remember it?

ROB'S GRANDFATHER. I was only six, but I knew something was up. My father worked for the longshoremen's union—

NEVA. You were the only boy I'd ever met who'd read *Pride and Prejudice* more than once.

ROB. And you were the only girl I'd ever met who's named after a Russian river and who can play the Bach unaccompanied flute sonata.

NEVA. I was just lucky I got you before Ann Philanders did.

ROB *(reading)*. "We only broadcast an hour or two at a time, with no set schedule. Out of paranoia about being discovered, we'd only told friends about the station, but we wanted to be heard by more than a few high-school students. We put up an inconspicuous card on a couple of record-shop bulletin boards with our call letters and frequency. We were so hungry to know we were being listened to that we went a step farther: we announced my number over the air and asked listeners to call in with feedback.

ZAD. This is KPOW. *(Sound of explosion.)* Your anarchist alternative, with the Z Man at the pirate helm.

ROB *(reading)*. "Neva printed up QSL cards to mail out. We waited. Three broadcasts passed. Then four. Not a single call from a stranger came in. We began almost to hope that the FCC was at least listening."

ROB'S GRANDFATHER. And even if they hear you, it's not like you're interfering with some megastation.

NEVA. The worst they'd probably do is take away the equipment.

ZAD. And kill themselves getting the antenna off the roof.

ROB *(reading)*. "Of all the holidays in the pirate radio year, Halloween is number one. We decided to go on at nine p.m. and do five straight hours, which is taking a chance. It was a Saturday. My mom and Andy had gone up the coast for the night. Everyone came over and Zad kicked us off with a group called Beyond the Fringe."

ZAD. —comedy that's so fast and so British you have *no clue* what's actually happening.

ROB *(reading)*. "We gave the phone number and asked listeners to call in. Friends called and said reception was strong. I read some E.E. Cummings, Pinsky, Rimbaud.

Neva was doing a piece on the sweatshops down on Third Street when the phone rang again."

ZAD. First, he said he really liked the show. Then he said his name was Agent something-or-other and asked if I wanted a corner prison cell or an aisle. Then he asked for you.

ROB *(reading)*. "It was too noisy, so I took the call in my parents' room. The guy said that I had a good radio voice. I remember being impressed with myself."

LENNY. And I'm not saying that just because I'm your father.

ROB *(reading)*. "I was struck speechless. I shut the door and lay down on the bed."

LENNY. I've been visiting back out here for a week. First time in a long time. So I thought I'd give you a call. Believe it or not, I think about you a lot. *(The sound-effects recording rises into hearing and plays behind the rest of the scene.)* Back when you were three or four, I had a boy your age living next door, and I'd look at him and think, that's something like what you must look like. Riding a Big Wheel, making car sounds. Everywhere I lived, there was always someone I could watch.

BOY ROB. "The capital of Louisiana is Baton Rouge—"

ROB'S GRANDFATHER. What's the difference between an accordion and an onion?

ROB'S GRANDMOTHER. We give up.

ROB'S GRANDFATHER. No one cries when you chop up an accordion.

LENNY. You still there?

ROB. Yeah.

LENNY. Anyway, Rob—Jessica told me you go by "Rob." I couldn't find your mother in the book. And her folks must be unlisted. But I finally tracked down Jessica. She filled me in on things and about Rose being married, and said you'd be on the radio tonight. I really just wanted to hear your voice. But then when you gave the number it seemed crazy for us not to talk. At least for a minute. If you want.

MALE RADIO ANNOUNCER. —her famous aria "*Un bel di*," describing in detail how Pinkerton will one day sail into the harbor—

LENNY. Don't worry. I'm not coming over. She wouldn't even tell me where you're living. Just hearing your voice is enough of a thrill.

BOY ROB. "In spite of all their friends could say,
     On a winter's morn, on a stormy day—"

LENNY. It sounds like Rose has been great for a mother, which I knew she would be. And that her husband's a good guy. Which I'm glad for. I really am.

ROB *(reading)*. "Here was my chance. To ask him anything I wanted. To blast him. To tell him how I'd tracked him through the airwaves, how I'd done all my school reports on Louisiana in his honor, how I knew his face and habits and brand of accordion but that he'd never bothered to learn the first thing about me. *(Pause.)* But the words weren't waiting on my tongue, as they'd once been."

LENNY. And I don't blame you for whatever you think about me. I'm sure it's not good. And I'm sure I deserve it. If I could have sent money to help out, I sure would have. *(Pause.)* Hearing you on the air gave me a feeling I don't think you'd believe. To think that you're doing radio. *(Pause.)* Can I ask you a question?

ROB. Go ahead.

LENNY. I'd just like to ask… Do you hate me? *(A longer pause, the silence occupied by the calls on the sound effects recording.)*

ROB. I used to.

LENNY. What about now?

ROB. I don't know. It's like you're more like a stranger. Not really connected to my life. I really don't think about you anymore.

LENNY. Would you like me to be…more connected?

ROB. Not really.

LENNY. Not in person. I could maybe just call, just every once in a while.

ROB *(reading)*. "'On the Air' should have been on his coat of arms. He was a voice without a body. A creature of air. A true radio man."

LENNY. Just on the telephone.

ROB. I'm happy with my life the way it is. And the people in it.

LENNY *(pause)*. That's good to hear, Rob. I'm glad for you. Say. Did you get the record and the tape I left you when you were a baby?

BOY ROB. Makes your wallpaper change right there on the wall—

FEMALE RADIO ANNOUNCER. —the coolest place on the dial—KWKH, Shreveport.

ROB. Yeah.

LENNY. Good. I always wondered about that.

ROB *(reading)*. "I almost asked him where he was, but didn't."

LENNY. I'll let you get back to business. It's been great hearing you.

ROB *(reading)*. "And he hung up." *(The swamp sounds gradually fade out.)*

ANDY. You're kneeling. Your arms are at your sides, very loose.

ROB *(reading)*. "I lay on the bed. After a minute I rolled onto the floor and got into the fallen leaf."

ANDY. Your hands are pointing behind you. Palms are up.

ROB *(reading)*. "How strange it all was. He'd felt justified in abandoning a child he'd never asked for; I'd felt righteous in my longing for his attention. All these years later, he was ready for a relationship, by which time I no longer missed him. We were riding a seesaw, facing each other up or down."

BOY ROB. What does it mean? The words are in French.

ROB'S MOTHER. Such a beautiful song, but the words are sad. The man says he woke up in the morning and that he sat on his bed and cried.

BOY ROB. How come?

ROB'S MOTHER. Because he had a dream about the woman he loves, who has the little black eyes. She's gone, and he's never going to see her again.

ROB *(reading)*. "What had brought on his call? A terminal disease? A surge of longing for a son? Guilt snowballing down the decades? Mere curiosity? Why hadn't I asked him? I knew I'd seemed cold. He'd probably taken my unresponsiveness for revenge: Me rejecting him with silence, payment for the seventeen years' dead air I'd received from him. But the old accusations felt like another character's lines. I hadn't been positive, when I'd put his box in the attic, whether I'd actually changed or just convinced myself I had. Now I knew."

ROB'S MOTHER. Like crossing the equator—invisible, but real.

ANDY. Now close your eyes. Try to slow down your breathing.

ROB *(reading)*. "The call had been an earthquake, an unexpected jolt. But my walls hadn't collapsed. The fallen leaf is the most stable of shapes. This time, I felt I hadn't simply twisted my unwilling limbs into it, but that I possessed it within me."

NEVA. I was reading on the air. I had no idea—

ROB'S MOTHER. I can't believe Jessica didn't prepare you.

ROB. She did. She left a message on the machine, but with everything going on to get ready for the broadcast, I didn't play it till today.

ROB'S MOTHER. Where's he living?

ROB. I don't know.

AUNT JUNE. What's he doing for work?

ROB. Don't know.

ROB'S MOTHER. Is he married?

ROB. Didn't ask.

ROB'S MOTHER. I wish I'd been here.

ROB. Actually, you were. In the Whispering Gallery.

(We hear the swamp sounds before, during and after LENNY's excerpt.)

LENNY. —my last show here at "The Ghost Raising," so I'm gonna go out with my own request. Which I'm sending out to a new listener, Robert Allan Radkovitz, pretty newly arrived in the world. Robert, this sweet Cajun waltz is for you, the same way it was for your mother. And from what I hear, you've got the looks that fit it, so here it is—"Little Black Eyes," played here by—

ROB *(reading)*. "It's been six months since the call. Life, as I'd told Lenny, is quite sufficiently full and fulfilling. We're still doing broadcasts on KPOW. I'm working on a short story I want to read at the next writers' group meeting. I'll be going to Reed College in Portland in the fall, and to a writing workshop in Vermont this summer with Neva."

ROB'S MOTHER. I was young and Lenny was younger.

ROB *(reading)*. "On my part, I've realized that when I was conceived Lenny was only seven years older than I am now. It's hard to imagine that kind of responsibility at that age. I've also done some thinking about how lucky I've been with the family that raised me."

ROB'S GRANDMOTHER. I'd love it. You're a dear, Robbie. The Agatha Christie, on the dresser. I like your voice so much better than the one on the tape.

ROB *(reading)*. "I also find myself wondering about the answers to all the questions I never asked him. I have no way to contact him—this time, by my own doing. I wonder if he'll seek me out in the future. It wouldn't surprise me, since he has the number. Halloween, when the spirits return to earth for one night, comes around every year."

LENNY. Making the dead one's favorite foods. That's what brings 'em back home.

ROB *(reading)*. "Maybe, some year, I'll even make gumbo."

(The swamp sounds come up, then gradually fade out. Curtain.)